Songs and chants for teaching spelling

SINGING SPELLING

Helen MacGregor
and Stephen Chadwick

ball

ice cream

fish

boat

Eve

sandcastle

bucket

sand

Singalong CD

Musical fun to support spelling

CONTENTS

2 SINGING SPELLING © HELEN MACGREGOR & STEPHEN CHADWICK 2011, A&C BLACK PUBLISHERS LTD

First published 2011 by A&C Black Publishers Ltd
Bloomsbury Publishing Plc, 49–51 Bedford Square, London, WC1B 3DP

Copyright © Helen MacGregor, Stephen Chadwick 2011
CD - A&C Black 2011

ISBN: 978-1-4081-40871

Printed by Caligraving Ltd, Thetford, Norfolk

Edited by Stephanie Matthews
Designed by Fi Grant
Cover illustration © Sandra Isaksson 2011
Inside illustrations © Emily Skinner 2011
CD produced by Stephen Chadwick
Performed by Debbie Sanders and Nigel Pilkington

This book is produced using paper that is made from wood grown in managed, sustainable forests. It is natural, renewable and recyclable. The logging and manufacturing processes confirm to the environmental regulations of the country of origin.

INTRODUCTION

Singing Spelling is a songbook full of stimulating and fun songs, games and chants designed to support the teaching of literacy and spelling for 7-9 year olds.

The songs provide opportunities for aural, visual and kinaesthetic learning which help promote the understanding and memorisation of letters, phonemes, and spelling patterns and rules. Through active involvement in the songs and related activities, the children will experience and explore a wide range of vocabulary using alliteration, rhyme, sequence and pattern. The rhythms and melodies of the songs give the vocabulary an extra dimension – a tried and tested way of promoting enjoyment and helping with memory skills and recall.

Links to the DfE Support for Spelling strategy document

All the songs are linked with the DfE Support for Spelling strategy but can also be used with any scheme. They can be used either with a whole class or with smaller groups in focused group work. Select the songs in the order of your choice to complement your teaching plans.

The Singing Spelling Songs

Some of the songs have familiar, traditional melodies and new lyrics. There are also new chants and songs with original melodies in contemporary styles. A photocopiable lyrics sheet is provided for each song. The melody lines for all songs can be found on pages 50-62.

The CD

Each of the songs in **Singing Spelling** has a lively, fun performance track and a backing track (see full track listings on the inside front cover of the book). The CD icons at the top of each activity give the track numbers (see below).

 CD track number

Use the performance track to teach the song to the class or to learn it yourself, if you prefer to teach the song first using your own voice. Once the children are confident, they can perform without the recorded vocal trackby singing with the backing track.

Resources

The 'What you will need' box lists any resources which are needed for any activity. A selection of letter cards are included on pages 63-64 which can be used for several of the activities.

Teaching focus

The Teaching focus of each song can be found at the bottom of each page

About the activities

Using the songs

The accompanying teaching notes for each song give step-by-step suggestions for effective ways to introduce each song to the children. It is recommended that the children learn the songs aurally, though you may wish to show them the photocopiable lyrics sheets at a later stage to investigate spellings or to develop their reading skills.

The songs and chants in **Singing Spelling** can be used in a variety of different ways and are designed so that literacy can easily be integrated into cross-curricular work. Use the ideas in the 'Extend the activities' section to create more challenging development activities. Many of these provide ideas for the children to work creatively and allow differentiation at different levels. Songs can be revisited at a later date to consolidate the children's learning.

Songs for games

These simple songs and chants provide a structure for playing games which the teacher can adapt to suit the needs of the class or particular groups of children. Once the children have learnt the game using the example on the CD, the teacher can select and substitute words appropriate to the children's levels of development to play the game at different times to reinforce their learning. An example of this can be seen in Phoneme Spotter where the children sort words selected by the teacher into short and long vowel sounds, either aurally or by reading word cards.

Songs for exploring spelling

As the children learn the songs, they will experience a range of key vocabulary in a memorable context. The extension activities give ideas for encouraging the children to explore further vocabulary by composing their own lyrics. In this way, teachers can set tasks to suit the level of their pupils and to extend their learning, eg, in Busy Kitchen, the children learn to perform a sequence of onomatopaeic words, then compose a new rap which they can perform with the backing track.

Songs as an aide-memoire

Some songs serve to memorise spelling rules, eg, in Words to Remember, the children learn the spelling rule for verbs ending with -e: 'drop the -e, add -ing'. In the activity, they find other verbs which follow this rule to make up a new set of verses to sing with the backing track.

Extend the activities

Each song has an accompanying set of extension notes which give more ideas of how you can use the song, adding more breadth and depth to the children's learning of vocabulary, eg, in Cinderella, the children can replace the adjectives in the lyrics with others of their own choice. Many of the extension ideas move from aural work to the development of reading and writing.

ALPHABET

Using the song

★ Show the class either the lower or the upper case alphabet display.

★ Listen to the song (track 1), pointing to each letter in turn to familiarise the children with the letter names and the sequence as it builds up in the song. All practise together, saying the letters one by one.

★ Play the track again and sing the alphabet letters together when they appear in the song.

★ Introduce the other lines of the song once the children have sung the alphabet letters though several times.

★ When the children are confident with all the lyrics, sing along together with the backing track (track 2). Invite a conductor to point to the letters as you sing.

Extend the activities

★ Give out an individual alphabet letter card to each child (if you have more than twenty-six children, some will need to share letters between them). Sing the song slowly, without the backing track. As each letter is sung, the child with the matching card holds up the letter for everyone to see.

★ Swap cards and repeat. Can the children do this while singing with the backing track?

★ Give the children plenty of opportunities to use the letters both orally and in writing, eg, by spelling their names orally and making name labels, using capital letters as appropriate.

★ In pairs or small groups, play 'Snap' with the alphabet cards using lower, upper or a mixture of cases to match your children's stage of learning. Name the letters out loud as the cards are placed down and shout 'Snap!' when two letters match.

★ Extend the game by making it a rule that each child thinks of a word beginning with their letter as they place the card on the table.

What you will need

- A large display of the alphabet in lower and upper case

- For the extension activity: sets of individual letter cards in lower and upper case

TEACHING FOCUS

• Letters and sequence of the alphabet

ALPHABET

Say the alphabet with me,
A B C D.
Keep to the beat and you will see,
A B C D E F G.
Learning the alphabet is easy!
A B C D E F G
H I J K L M N O P.
Stay cool and use your head,
You start at A and end at Z!
A B C D E F G
H I J K L M N O P
Q R S T U V W
X Y Z.

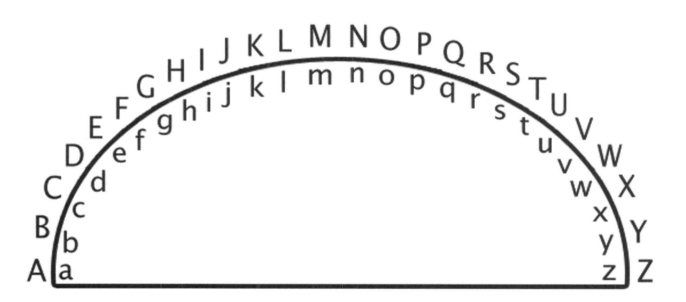

PHONEME SPOTTER

Using the song

★ Learn how to play the Phoneme Spotter game by listening to the song (track 3). Listen out for examples of short or long vowel words.

★ Teach the children the lyrics of the sung section ('Short vowel, long vowel'), then play the game, selecting your own short or long vowel words for them to identify. Call these out one by one in the chanted section so that the children can respond with their answers.

★ Rather than calling out the answers, you may prefer the children to indicate them with a hand gesture: hands close together for short vowels, hands wide apart for long vowels, so that you can see if anyone is having difficulties with the game.

★ Play the game aurally at first, then investigate the written spelling patterns.

★ Introduce a wider variety of short and long vowel phonemes by using the backing track (track 4) and replacing the words from the teaching track with your own selections. Use word cards with the new words as a point of discussion after the children have aurally sorted the words into short or long vowel sounds.

Extend the activities

★ The children can work with partners to sort sets of common words with a particular phoneme. One child chooses a card and calls out the word for their partner to write down. They then check their spelling using the card.

★ Take it in turns with the other cards. Can they list all the different ways of spelling the phoneme, eg, make, away, train, name, paper and great?

What you will need

- Word cards with examples of short and long vowel sounds

TEACHING FOCUS

- Short and long vowel phonemes

PHONEME SPOTTER

Short vowel, long vowel,
Short or long?
Here's the answer after this song:
Dad: short.
Mum: short.
Gran: short.
Babe: long.

Short vowel, long vowel,
Short or long?
Here's the answer after this song:
Me: long.
You: long.
Us: short.
Them: short.

SPELLING HOKEY COKEY*

Using the song

★ Prepare the letter cards you will need to spell the words try, pie, nice and sigh.

★ Play the song (track 5), demonstrating to the class how to spell each word by holding up the letter cards to match the instructions in the lyrics.

★ Play the track again and sing the song together. Discuss the different ways of spelling the long 'i' sound in each of the verses.

★ You may like to ask the children to write the words on individual whiteboards as you sing the song together.

Extend the activities

★ Use the model of the song to practise spelling other long words with the 'i' vowel sound, eg, cry, lie, nine, time.

★ Substitute the 'i' vowel sound with other long vowel spelling patterns:

- 'Ai': day, say, play, make, bake, rain, sail.
- 'Ee': see, bee, sea, read.
- 'Oa': toe, low, show, soap, boat, note, home.
- 'Oo': use, new, blue, chew, huge, tune, glue.

★ Order the lyrics according to the first letter of each word, eg, verse 1: read – 'You put the letter r first and then the e, a too', 'You finish with the letter d...'; then verse 2: tune; verse 3: use etc.

★ There is a phonics version of this song in Singing Phonics 2, pgs 12–13 (ISBN: 9781408114513) that uses the phonemes to construct words rather than spelling the words out using letter names. Note that this earlier stage could be used instead.

*Thanks to the Infants staff of Woodchurch Primary school, Kent for the idea for this adaptation.

What you will need

- Individual letter cards
- Individual whiteboards (optional)

TEACHING FOCUS

- Long 'i' vowel sound and other long vowel spelling patterns

SPELLING HOKEY COKEY
Tune: The Hokey Cokey

You put the letter t first and then the letter r too,
You finish with the letter y and give a yoo hoo hoo!
You put them all together and you wait and see,
What will the new word be?
Oh, we can spell a new word... (x3)
t – r – y spells try, you see.

You put the letter p first and then the letter i too,
You finish with the letter e and give a yoo hoo hoo!
You put them all together and you wait and see,
What will the new word be?
Oh, we can spell a new word... (x3)
p – i – e spells pie, you see.

You put the letter n first and then the letter i too,
You finish with a c and e and give a yoo hoo hoo!
You put them all together and you wait and see,
What will the new word be?
Oh, we can spell a new word... (x3)
n – i – c – e spells nice, you see.

You put the letter s first and then the letter i too,
You finish with a g and h and give a yoo hoo hoo!
You put them all together and you wait and see,
What will the new word be?
Oh, we can spell a new word... (x3)
s – i – g – h spells sigh, you see.

11

SILENT LETTERS

Using the song

★ Play the song (track 7) and join in with the repeated lines in each verse and the chorus as they become familiar.

★ Teach the sequence of silent letters by showing the letter cards as you sing lines three and four of the chorus.

★ Ask the children to identify the silent letter used in the lyrics of each verse and to point out where it occurs in each of the words.

★ Display the lyrics so that they can check their answers and see all the spelling patterns.

★ When the song is familiar, perform it with the backing track (track 8).

Extend the activities

★ Working in pairs, individually or in small groups, the children can compose new verses using lyrics with the silent letters k, b, h and g, eg, 'At school rhinos rhyme in rhythm'.

★ Perform the new lyrics with the backing track.

★ Investigate other silent letters and compose some new verses using the new lyrics, eg, w, l, t and c:

- Wrists will wriggle when you write
- Folk feel calm beneath a palm
- Listen to the whistle in the castle
- Escalators descend and ascend

What you will need

- Letter cards for k, b, h and g

TEACHING FOCUS

- Silent letters and alliteration

SILENT LETTERS
Tune: She'll be coming round the mountain

Chorus:
Oh, you can't hear silent letters in some words. (No, you can't.)
Oh, you can't hear silent letters in some words. (No, you can't.)
There's a silent k and b,
Silent h and g,
Oh, you can't hear silent letters in some words. (No, you can't.)

Knock-kneed knight knows how to knit,
Knock-kneed knight knows how to knit,
Knock-kneed knight, knock-kneed knight,
Knock-kneed knight knows how to knit.

Don't eat crumbs with a numb thumb,
Don't eat crumbs with a numb thumb,
Don't eat crumbs, don't eat crumbs,
Don't eat crumbs with a numb thumb.

Chorus

What, where, when and which and why?...

Gnomes love gnawing naughty gnats...

Chorus

SINGING SPELLING © HELEN MACGREGOR & STEPHEN CHADWICK 2011, A&C BLACK PUBLISHERS LTD

SNAP, CRACKLE, POP!

Using the song

★ Listen to the song (track 9) together. Ask the children what they notice about the words of the repeated lines in each verse (they all start with the same sound and they are alliterative). What happens in the last verse? (The lines and sounds are sung in sequence.)

★ Learn to sing the verses one at a time using the voice expressively to articulate the snap, crackle and pop sounds at the end of each one.

★ Sing the song with the backing track (track 10) when the children are confident.

Extend the activities

★ Ask the children to invent their own alliterative lines, using their first names, to make new verses, eg, Ahmed is an amazing acrobat; Ben bought a big, blue barracuda.

★ To give the children practice at hearing and understanding that the same initial phoneme in words may be spelt in a variety of ways, encourage them to do this activity aurally at first. Once they have a phrase that uses words starting with the same sound, they can find out how to write down their phrases.

TEACHING FOCUS

• Alliteration

SNAP, CRACKLE, POP!

Cool Kate pulls Christmas crackers,
Cool Kate pulls Christmas crackers,
Cool Kate pulls Christmas crackers,
Snap, snap, snap!

Fred lets off fantastic fireworks,
Fred lets off fantastic fireworks,
Fred lets off fantastic fireworks,
Crackle, crackle, crackle!

Pradip's popping party poppers,
Pradip's popping party poppers,
Pradip's popping party poppers,
Pop, pop, pop!

Christmas crackers, snap, snap!
Fantastic fireworks, crackle, crackle!
Party poppers, pop, pop!
Snap, crackle, pop!

HUBBLE BUBBLE

(11) (12)

Using the song

★ Listen to the song (track 11) together. Play it again, asking the children to join in with the male and female voices singing the second phrase of each line, eg, 'hubble hubble bubble'.

★ Practise singing the sequence of the words in each line, then sing the whole song when the children are familiar with the lyrics.

★ Invent some simple actions to go with each line, eg, 'hubble bubble' – wiggling fingers; 'double trouble' – wagging both index fingers.

Extend the activities

★ Working in pairs or small groups invent new sequences of two lines using words with -le endings, eg, 'Prickle trickle, prickle prickle trickle'; 'Scribble dribble, scribble scribble dribble'.

★ The children can add their own actions to accompany the verses and practise by repeating their verse five times with the backing track (track 12).

★ Ask five groups to take it in turns to perform their ideas with the backing track.

TEACHING FOCUS

• Words with -le ending

HUBBLE BUBBLE

Hubble bubble, hubble hubble bubble,
Double trouble, double double trouble.

Tickle chuckle, tickle tickle chuckle,
Giggle wriggle, giggle giggle wriggle.

Wibble wobble, wibble wibble wobble,
Sniffle snuffle, sniffle sniffle snuffle.

Stumble tumble, stumble stumble tumble,
Rumble grumble, rumble rumble grumble.

Sizzle fizzle, sizzle sizzle fizzle,
Frazzle dazzle, frazzle frazzle dazzle.

ANIMAL SYLLABLES

13 **14**

Using the song

★ Explain to the children that syllables are 'chunks' of words based around the vowel sounds that are heard when the words are spoken.

★ Play the song (track 13) and join in together with the repeat of the first two lines. Join in with the chorus as it becomes familiar.

★ As you are learning the song, discuss the animals listed in each verse and clap each syllable in the animal words as you practise saying them.

★ Perform the whole song with the backing track (track 14).

Extend the activities

★ Find pictures of other animals and ask the children to identify the number of syllables in their names. Substitute these in the appropriate verse of the song, eg, rat (one syllable), beaver (two syllables), elephant (three syllables). Investigate animal names with more than three syllables, eg, alligator (four), hippopotamus (five).

★ Extend the song by writing verses with a new subject, eg, names of minibeasts or names of boys and girls.

TEACHING FOCUS

• Recognition of syllables

ANIMAL SYLLABLES

Names of animals with one syllable,
Cat, pig, bear and snake.
Names of animals with one syllable,
Cat, pig, bear and snake.

Chorus:
One, two, three,
How many syllables will there be?
One, two, three or four,
Some words have even more!

Names of animals with two syllables,
Rabbit, monkey, badger and lion.
Names of animals with two syllables,
Rabbit, monkey, badger and lion.

Chorus

Names of animals with three syllables,
Kangaroo, crocodile, chimpanzee,
And that's three!
Kangaroo, crocodile, chimpanzee,
And that's three!

BUSY KITCHEN

(15) (16)

Using the song

★ Teach the children the kitchen sounds one at a time by playing the Busy Kitchen game. When you call out the name of each kitchen appliance, the children respond with the matching sound words, adding appropriate actions.

★ Encourage them to use their voices expressively to say the sound words.

★ Gradually build up the calls, saying them in a random order, until the children know all the responses and can respond promptly.

★ Choose individual children to lead the game.

★ Show the children the lyrics and discuss the word endings used: -sh, -ow and -ing. Now teach the sequence of the rap by listening to the song (track 15).

★ When the children are familiar with the lyrics, perform the song together with the backing track (track 16).

Extend the activities

★ Invent a new call and response game to explore other sound words, eg, transport sounds, animal sounds and environmental sounds. Small groups can select and sequence their own lyrics to create a performance. Invite them to perform these to the class with the backing track.

TEACHING FOCUS

• Word endings - sh, -ow, -ing
• Onomatopoeia

BUSY KITCHEN

Call: Dish wash, dish wash,
Response: Splish splosh, splish splosh!

Call: Washing machine,
Response: Swish swash, swish swash!

Call: Electric toaster,
Response: Glow glow, glow pop!

Call: Hob extractor fan,
Response: Blow blow, blow stop!

Call: Oven timer,
Response: Tick tock, ting!

Call: Microwave oven,
Response: Ping!

swish
swash

glow glow

ping! ping!

EVERYONE

Using the song

★ Listen to the song together (track 17) and discuss the children's thoughts about the meaning of the lyrics and some of the issues referred to: drought, famine, homelessness, bullying and caring for others.

★ Ask the children to identify what is similar about the lyrics of each verse (the form of words in the first lines, the alternating repeated second line, the -ight rhymes at the end of the second and last lines).

★ Display the lyrics where everyone can see them and use them to learn the song one verse at a time.

★ When the children know the whole song, divide the class into three groups. Each group sings a different word from the first line, then all the groups join together for the rest of the verse.

★ When the children are confident, perform the whole song with the backing track (track 18).

Extend the activities

★ Invite the children to identify all the compound words in the song and say these out loud together.

★ Play Pairs:

1) Give small groups a set of cards each showing the individual words they need to make the twelve compound words in the first lines of each verse (see What you will need box).

2) Place all the cards face down on the table and invite each child to take turns to reveal two words.

3) When they can place two cards together to form a compound word from the song, the new words are taken out of play to make a list at the side of the table. If the two cards selected do not create a compound word they should be placed back, face down on the table.

4) The game is complete when all twelve words are formed.

★ Look at the spelling pattern of the words right, night, bright, light. Can the children think of other words which include the letters igh, eg, fight, tight, might, sight, high, height? Encourage them to use the words in whole sentences.

★ Compare this spelling pattern with rhyming words using the split vowel digraph i-e: white, site, kite, bite.

What you will need

- An enlarged copy of the lyrics
- For the extension activity: sets of word cards: every, no, some, any (three of each in a set); one, body, where (four of each in a set)

TEACHING FOCUS

- High frequency compound words
- Words with -igh spelling pattern

EVERYONE

Everyone, everybody, everywhere,
Every day, every night,
Needs shelter from the cold, food and water,
It's a basic human right.

No-one, nobody, nowhere,
In the day or the night,
Should be afraid or hurt, or feel that nothing
In life can ever be bright. Oh yeah!

Someone, somebody, somewhere,
Every day, every night,
Is helping other people when they need it,
To make them feel all right.

Anyone, anybody, anywhere,
In the day or the night,
Can help to feed the homeless, cold and hungry,
Can care and bring some light. Oh yeah!

Everyone, everybody, everywhere,
Every day, every night.

LOOK, SAY, COVER, WRITE, CHECK

Using the song

★ Talk to the class about the strategy for learning how to spell unfamiliar or polysyllabic words: Look, say, cover, write and check.

★ Listen to the song (track 19) together. Teach the children the mnemonic chant (LSCWC) then encourage them to join in with the first and third lines of the chorus.

★ Learn the verses together and when the children are confident, sing the whole song with the backing track (track 20).

★ The children may like to add finger-spelling actions to represent the letters LSCWC.

Extend the activities

★ Working in small groups or with the whole class if you prefer, introduce selected words using flashcards or display them on an interactive whiteboard.

★ Sing the chorus of the song to remind the children of the strategy, then ask them to say each word from the flashcards/interactive whiteboard out loud.

★ Conceal the word and ask them to write it down, then check it, discussing any useful ways to help memorise the spellings accurately.

What you will need

- For the extension activity: flashcards or an interactive whiteboard
- Individual whiteboards or pencils and paper

TEACHING FOCUS

- Strategy for learning new spellings

LOOK, SAY, COVER, WRITE, CHECK

Tune: Yankee Doodle

(Chant)
LSCWC
LSCWC

When you want to learn the way to spell a certain word,
Sing this song and use this plan, the best I've ever heard:

Chorus:
Look, say, cover, write and check.
(Don't forget to check it!)
Look, say, cover, write and check,
I'm sure you won't regret it!

(Chant)
LSCWC
LSCWC

Use your eyes and use your brain, then write the letters out,
Check the word, you'll soon improve — of this I have no doubt!

Chorus

(Chant)
LSCWC
LSCWC

Use your phonics, break it down, turn letters into sounds.
Memorise and it will help next time you write it down.

Chorus

RHYME RAP

Using the song

★ Using the song (track 21), learn the chorus first then listen to each verse.

★ Learn the verses aurally, one by one, adding actions to help memorise each sequence of rhyming words.

★ When the children are familiar with the words, use a large display of the lyrics to discuss the various spelling patterns of the rhymes, eg, train, plane.

Extend the activities

★ Ask the children to suggest other rhyming words and then use them to make new verses to be performed with the backing track (track 22). They can work in pairs or small groups to create their own versions to perform to the class.

★ Use word cards to play 'I spy'. Adapt the song as follows:

Rhyme, rhyme, look at words that rhyme,

Use your eyes and keep in time.

Rhyme, rhyme, look at words that rhyme,

Use your eyes and keep in time.

I see with my little eye,

Something that rhymes with...

★ Show the children a set of word cards (see What you will need box). Can they recognise the rhyming words to sing the third line of the verse?

What you will need

- I spy extension activity: three sets of word cards with rhyming words and one or two cards with non-rhyming words, eg, grow, flow, mow, bow, show, milk, boy

TEACHING FOCUS

- Rhyme
- Exploring spelling patterns

 SINGING SPELLING © HELEN MACGREGOR & STEPHEN CHADWICK 2011, A&C BLACK PUBLISHERS LTD

RHYME RAP

Chorus:
Rhyme, rhyme, listen to the rhyme,
Stay cool and keep in time.
Rhyme, rhyme, listen to the rhyme,
Stay cool and keep in time.

I hear with my little ear,
Something that rhymes with cat.
Hat, rat, fat and splat,
Words that rhyme with cat.

Chorus

I hear with my little ear,
Something that rhymes with tap.
Cap, snap, flap and clap,
Words that rhyme with tap.

Chorus

I hear with my little ear,
Something that rhymes with rain.
Train, plane, brain and pain,
Words that rhyme with rain.

Chorus

FEEL OKAY

Using the song

★ Listen to the song (track 23) and ask the children to share any of the words they remember. Can they group the rhyming words? Do they notice anything about the lyrics (many of the words end in -le).

★ Teach the song by encouraging the children to join in with all the repeated vocabulary first, then learn the whole phrase in each line. Focus on encouraging the children to clearly articulate the consonants in each word.

★ Sing the song with the backing track (track 24) when the children are confident.

Extend the activities

★ Ask children to group all the words with -le endings into the following three categories:

- Short vowel, double consonant (same): puddle, muddle, giggle, niggle, wiggle, battle, rattle, tittle, tattle, struggle.

- Short vowel, double consonant (different): grumble, stumble, jumble.

- Long vowel, single consonant: doodle, noodle, poodle.

★ Once the children are familiar with these three types of -le endings, play Find Your Team to explore further vocabulary:

1) Appoint three captains and give each of them a word card from each of the -le endings categories (examples are given in the box opposite). Stick a second copy of the word card to their backs.

2) Randomly distribute word cards from the three categories to the remaining children.

4) On 'Go' the captains search for their corresponding team members belonging to one of the three particular spelling patterns, eg, apple, purple, needle.

6) At the same time, the children check their words to find the correct captain.

What you will need

- Find Your Team extension activity: word cards from each of the three -le endings categories listed in the box below.
- Copies of each word card that can be stuck on children's backs
- Tape to attach the word cards to the children's backs

Find Your Team game card examples:

- Short vowel, double consonant (same): apple, middle, cattle, bottle, paddle.

- Short vowel, double consonant (different): purple, bundle, uncle, circle, handle, candle, single.

- Long vowel, single consonant: needle, people, steeple, beetle, eagle.

TEACHING FOCUS

- Rhyme
- -le word endings

FEEL OKAY

Don't grumble if you stumble,
Don't grumble if you stumble,
Don't grumble if you stumble and ev'rything's a jumble,
If you step in a puddle, or get yourself in a muddle,
Don't grumble! Don't grumble! Why don't you...
Just have a little giggle?   Giggle   giggle.
Don't let it niggle.   Niggle   niggle   niggle.
Give your toes a wiggle.   Wiggle   wiggle.
Give your toes a wiggle.
And you'll feel okay!

Don't battle if you're rattled,
Don't battle if you're rattled,
Don't battle if you're rattled when your friends tittle-tattle,
If you feel work's a struggle or it's a bit of a puzzle,
Don't battle! Don't battle! Why don't you...
Draw a little doodle?   Doodle   doodle.
Don't be a noodle.   Noodle   noodle   noodle.
Go and pat a poodle.   Poodle   poodle.
Go and pat a poodle.
And you'll feel okay!

CINDERELLA

Using the song

★ Listen to the song (track 25) and look at an enlarged copy of the lyrics. Ask the children to identify all the adjectives, and then sort them into the following groups:

- those with the suffix -ful: wonderful, disgraceful, forgetful, joyful, beautiful, grateful.

- those with the suffix -less: careless, thoughtless, hopeless.

- those with prefixes: disgraceful, unkind(ness).

- other adjectives: ugly, royal, homely, kind, sly, bossy, rude, sad, magical, happy.

★ Learn the verses one at a time. Encourage the children to use their voices expressively to tell the story and emphasise the adjectives used in the lyrics.

★ Finally, perform the song to the backing track (track 26).

Extend the activities

★ Remind the children of the adjectives in the song which use prefixes and introduce them to other adjectives which use prefixes, eg, unhelpful, unselfish, disrespectful.

★ Replace the adjectives used in the song with new ones to write descriptions about Cinderella, her sisters, the fairy godmother and the Prince, eg, 'Cinderella was unselfish but her life was miserable'; 'Her sisters were unkind, spiteful, sly and unhelpful around the house'.

TEACHING FOCUS

- Rhyme
- Adjectives, suffixes and prefixes

CINDERELLA
Tune: On top of old smokey

We know Cinderella,
A wonderful tale
Of two ugly sisters
And a right royal male!

It's said Cinderella
Was homely and kind,
Worked hard for her sisters
But she didn't mind.

Her sisters were careless,
So thoughtless and sly.
At chores they were hopeless,
They just wouldn't try.

We know they were ugly,
Both bossy and rude,
Their manners disgraceful
As they ate their food.

They acted forgetful,
Never cleaned floors or walls,
But they always remembered
The parties and balls!

The fairy godmother
Changed Cinders' sad life,
And Cinders was joyful
As Prince Charming's wife.

She thanked all the creatures
And magical friends,
And we are all grateful
For the tale's happy end!

We prefer it when baddies
Don't get their own way.
No place for unkindness
At the end of the day!

QUESTIONS

Using the song

★ Listen to the song (track 27) to learn the chorus. Ask the children to identify the compound words used in each verse either by listening to the track or by looking at a copy of the lyrics:

- Verse 1: earthworm, football, underground, playtime, goalkeeper.

- Verse 2: ladybird, seaside, weekend, paintbrush, raincoat, sunhat.

- Verse 3: butterfly, birthday, bedtime.

★ Learn the verses and all sing the song with the backing track (track 28).

Extend the activities

★ Play the Compound Word game. Give individual word cards (see What you will need box) to small groups of children. Ask them to form as many compound words as they can using the individual word cards and make a list of the results, eg,

- Word cards: lady, black, bird, box, card, post, house, green, glass.

- Compound words: ladybird, blackbird, birdbox, postbox, postlady, postcard, greenhouse, glasshouse.

What you will need

- A set of individual word cards using the compound words from the song, eg, earth, worm, under, ground

TEACHING FOCUS

- Compound words

QUESTIONS
Tune: My bonnie lies over the ocean

I wonder if earthworms play football,
Deep down underground, in a hole?
D'you think that they ever have playtime?
Their goalkeeper could be a mole!

Chorus:
Questions, questions,
I dream them up when I'm in bed, in bed.
Questions, questions,
They buzz all around in my head.

Do ladybirds fly to the seaside,
To have a weekend in the sun?
Do they put on their spots with a paintbrush,
Wear raincoats and sunhats for fun?

Chorus

Oh, when is a butterfly's birthday?
Is the cake in the shape of her wings?
Does she blow out the candles at bedtime?
I wish I knew all of these things!

Chorus

PRESENT AND PAST

Using the song

★ Teach the children to play the Present and Past mime game. Check that the children understand that the present tense describes something that is happening now, and that the past tense describes something that has already happened. Learn the song (track 29).

★ When everyone is ready, sing the song together, choosing a confident child to mime an action during the song.

★ Ask the children to make up their own verses and present them to the class. At the end of the first verse the singers identify and describe the action in the present tense, and use the past tense at the end of verse two, eg, He's riding a bike; He rode a bike.

★ Discuss alternative forms of the tenses, eg, He rides a bike; He was riding a bike.

★ You might like the children to play this game in small groups, each taking a turn at miming an action, eg, playing a guitar, eating an ice cream or kicking a ball.

Extend the activities

★ Change the lyrics to 'Tell us what you are doing today/did yesterday'. Invite a confident child to sing a solo in the last line of each verse, using the present and past tenses.

TEACHING FOCUS

• Present and past tense

PRESENT AND PAST

Tune: Here we go round the Mulberry Bush

Show us what you're doing today,
Doing today, doing today,
Show us what you're doing today,
She's reading a book.

Every sentence should have a verb,
A doing word, yes, that's a verb,
Every sentence should have a verb,
And reading is present tense.

Show us what you did yesterday,
Did yesterday, did yesterday,
Show us what you did yesterday,
She read a book.

Every sentence should have a verb,
A doing word, yes, that's a verb,
Every sentence should have a verb,
And read is the past tense.

RECORD-BREAKING FOOD

(31) (32)

Using the song

★ Listen to the song (track 31). Talk about the use of the three comparative adjectives in each verse, eg, hot, hotter and hottest. What do the children notice about the last two lines of each verse? (They rhyme.)

★ Teach the lyrics one verse at a time, then perform the whole song with the backing track (track 32).

Extend the activities

★ Ask the children to find other comparative adjectives which have the same regular endings, eg, long, longer, longest; big, bigger, biggest; ripe, riper, ripest; rude, ruder, rudest.

★ Make up new verses using the children's suggestions and sing these with the backing track.

★ Look at the comparative forms of adjectives which end in 'y' to learn their spelling patterns (change the 'y' to 'i', then add the ending), eg, happy, happier, happiest; funny, funnier, funniest; silly, sillier, silliest).

★ Point out the irregular comparative forms of adjectives, eg, good, better, best and bad, worse, worst.

TEACHING FOCUS

• Adjectives
• Comparatives

RECORD-BREAKING FOOD

My curry's hot,
But could be hotter.
My curry's hot,
But could be hotter.
If I add a little sprinkle of some lovely chilli spice,
I'll have the hottest curry steaming on a bed of rice!

My cheese is old,
It's getting older.
My cheese is old,
It's getting older.
I can tell by all the maggots that it's really out of date,
I've got the oldest cheese and now it's wriggling off my plate!

My ice cream's cold,
But could be colder.
My ice cream's cold,
But could be colder.
If I send it to the Arctic to be buried in the snow,
I'll have the coldest ice cream, which will make your goosebumps grow!

My food is fast,
But could be faster.
My food is fast,
But could be faster.
If I shake and slap it in a bowl then microwave it quick,
I'll have the fastest food but then it may well look like sick!

DING DONG

(33) (34)

Using the song

★ Listen to the song (track 33) and try to join in together with the responses (eg, 'No, you don't.') when the argument sections are repeated the second time.

★ Teach the children the lyrics of each argument section, then practise performing them with the performance track (track 33).

★ Divide into two groups, allocating one part to each group. Swap parts for the repeat.

★ Show the children the lyrics for these two sections and discuss the use of the apostrophe to represent the missing letters in the abbreviated forms of do not, will not, are not, cannot. Point out the alternative abbreviations for 'you are not' – 'you aren't' (as used in the song) – and 'you're not'.

★ Learn the final verse and argument section of the song and sing these together in unison. When the children are confident, perform the song with the backing track (track 34).

Extend the activities

★ Investigate other tenses. Use the children's suggestions to make a new argument section for the song and perform this with the backing track, eg,

Yes, I was.	No, you weren't.
Yes, I could.	No, you couldn't.
Yes, I should.	No, you shouldn't.
Yes, I would.	No, you wouldn't.

★ Investigate other shortened forms of verbs which use the apostrophe, eg, I'm, he's, she's, you're, they're, I'll, you'll, I'd, I've. You may like to make up more choruses for the song using these too, eg, 'I'll go out. No, you won't'; 'You're a pest. No, I'm not!'

TEACHING FOCUS

• Verbs - using the apostrophe in shortened forms

DING DONG

My brother and I like to argue,
We argue all day long.
My Mum says: 'Here they go again —
Ding-dong, ding-dong, ding-dong!'

Yes, I do.   No, you don't.
Yes, I will.   No, you won't.
(Swap parts)
Yes, I do.   No, you don't.
Yes, I will.   No, you won't.

My brother tells me he's an expert,
I tell him that he's wrong.
My Mum says: 'Here they go again —
Ding-dong, ding-dong, ding-dong!'

Yes, I am.   No, you aren't.
Yes, I can.   No, you can't.
(Swap parts)
Yes, I am.   No, you aren't.
Yes, I can.   No, you can't.

But when we like to be friendly,
Play games or sing a song,
We say: 'Hey, no more arguing —
Ding-dong, ding-dong, ding-dong!'

Yes, we are.   Yes, we are.
Yes, we do.   Yes, we do.
(Swap parts)
Yes, we will.   Yes, we will.
You will too.   You will too.

STICK LIKE GLUE

Using the song

★ Ask the children how many words they can think of beginning with qu. Make a list of these and display the words where they can see them.

★ Listen to the song (track 35) and ask the children to join in with the echoes (performed by a male then female voice), identifying the qu words and highlighting them, or adding them to their list of suggestions.

★ Learn the whole song, then divide into two groups to sing the two parts in turn, joining together on the sections marked 'All' when both male and female voices sing on the performance track.

Extend the activities

★ Ask the children to work in small groups or pairs, using a dictionary, if needed, to find new words beginning with qu. They then choose four new qu words which they recognise to sing with the backing track (track 36).

★ Choose a group to perform their four choices, repeating them four times with the backing track while everyone sings the 'Q and u stick like glue' sections of the song.

★ Alternatively, choose three groups of children to each sing one qu word to create a sequence in the All section. You may also like to collect the words together to make a list of twelve qu-words in a selected order which everyone sings together.

TEACHING FOCUS

• Words beginning with qu

STICK LIKE GLUE

Group 1:   Q   Group 2: Q

Group 1: and u.   Group 2: and u.

All: Stick like glue.

Group 1: Q and u.   Group 2: Q and u.

All: Stick like glue.

All: Question, quiz, quick, quack.
Question, quiz, quick, quack.
Question, quiz, quick, quack.
Q and u stick like glue!

Group 1:   Q   Group 2: Q

Group 1: and u.   Group 2: and u.

All: Stick like glue.

Group 1: Q and u.   Group 2: Q and u.

All: Stick like glue.

DOUBLE TROUBLE

Using the song

★ Listen to the song (track 37) together. Divide the class into two groups to learn the verse section sung in two parts.

★ Add actions to match the words in the verses when the children are confident with the lyrics then all join in with the chorus.

★ Swap groups so that all the children have an opportunity to lead in the verse section.

★ Show the class an enlarged copy of the lyrics and discuss the rule. Can they suggest any more verbs that can be used to make new verses, eg, win, pat, chat, swim, shop, flop, rub, skip?

Extend the activities

★ Explore the spelling rule for the past tense of the verbs from the song. Repeat the song but this time Group 2 replaces the present tense with the past tense, ie clapped, tapped, hummed, drummed, hopped, stopped. Discuss the spelling rule, ie to change the present to the past tense, double the consonant and add -ed.

★ Explore other endings to create new versions of the song and perform these with the backing track (track 38), eg, double the consonant, add -er: swim/swimmer, win/winner, skip/skipper, rub/rubber; double the consonant, add 'y': chat/chatty, flop/floppy. Decide on new lyrics for the chorus as appropriate.

TEACHING FOCUS

• Verb endings (for verbs with one vowel before the final single consonant, double the consonant before adding the ending)

DOUBLE TROUBLE

Group 1:)
Clap clap clap.
Tap tap tap.
Hum hum hum.
Drum drum drum.
Hop hop hop.
Stop stop stop.

Group 2:
Clapping clapping clapping.
Tapping tapping tapping.
Humming humming humming.
Drumming drumming drumming.
Hopping hopping hopping.
Stopping stopping stopping.

Chorus:
If you want to end with -ing, double m or double p.
Double m or double p, if you want to end with -ing.
If you want to end with -ing, double m or double p.
Double m or double p, if you want to end with -ing.

Group 2:
Clap clap clap.
Tap tap tap.
Hum hum hum.
Drum drum drum.
Hop hop hop.
Stop stop stop.

Group 1:
Clapping clapping clapping.
Tapping tapping tapping.
Humming humming humming.
Drumming drumming drumming.
Hopping hopping hopping.
Stopping stopping stopping.

Chorus

WORDS TO REMEMBER

Using the song

★ Teach the chorus to the children ('Drop the 'e', add -ing').

★ Learn the first verse together and discuss how the lyrics relate to the chorus.

★ Give four children the letter cards required to spell out the first verb, 'make', and ask them to stand in line facing the class holding the cards up to make the word. Give another three children cards with the letters 'i', 'n' and 'g' and ask them to stand in order on the right of the first group, but with their backs to the class.

★ Sing the first verse of the song together (track 39). In line two, the child holding 'e' jumps back and the three -ing children turn and jump to the left to replace the 'e' card with the new ending.

★ Repeat the sequence for each verse using new letter cards.

★ Add dance actions to the last verse!

Extend the activities

★ Explore this spelling rule for other similar verbs with the children, eg, save, take, live, love, hate, dive, hope, care, bake, phone, rule, bite, rise, write, dance, arrive, scare, chase, freeze, excite, celebrate.

★ Ask the children to select five new verbs and substitute them for the ones in the song. Sing the song with the new verbs using the backing track (track 40).

★ Explore the spelling rule for the past tense of the verbs in the song and others, eg, saved, hated, hoped, arrived. Identify the irregular verbs: taken, frozen etc.

What you will need

- A set of lower case alphabet letter cards

TEACHING FOCUS

• Verbs using split vowel digraph drop the 'e' before adding the ending if the suffix starts with a vowel as in -ing

WORDS TO REMEMBER

Make is a verb which ends with 'e',
Drop the 'e', add -ing.
Making this and making that,
Making a word to remember!

Like is a verb which ends with 'e',
Drop the 'e', add -ing.
Liking this and liking that,
Liking a word to remember!

Drop the 'e', add -ing,
Drop the 'e', add -ing.

Use is a verb which ends with 'e',
Drop the 'e', add -ing.
Using this and using that,
Using a word to remember!

Change is a verb which ends with 'e',
Drop the 'e', add -ing.
Changing this and changing that,
Changing a word to remember!

Drop the 'e', add -ing,
Drop the 'e', add -ing.

Share is a verb which ends with 'e',
Drop the 'e', add -ing.
Sharing this and sharing that,
Sharing a word to remember!

SPELLING TRICKS

Using the song

★ Make a set of the word cards from the song (see What you will need box).

★ Play the song (track 41), holding up the matching pair of word cards (eg, hear and ear) for each verse.

★ Play the track again, asking the children to join in this time.

★ Talk about the spellings of each pair of words, noticing the words within words.

Extend the activities

★ Ask the children to make up more 'word within word' patterns which might help them remember spellings, eg, 'The monkey stole the key'; 'To get her, go together'; 'We found her here and there'. Perform the new verses with the backing track (track 42).

★ Teach the following word patterns to help memorise other tricky spelling patterns:

• 'Drink fruit juice, play guitar!' (-uit).

• 'Laugh And 'U' Get Happy!' (mnemonic).

• 'O, U Lucky Duck' (-ould endings as in could, would and should).

• Or better still, make up your own!

What you will need

• Make a set of word cards using the following words from the song: ear, hear, pie, piece, wear, hat, what, eight, height, weight, end, friend (see photocopiables pgs 63-64)

TEACHING FOCUS

• Memorising tricky spellings
• Words within words

SPELLING TRICKS

You hear it with your ear.
You hear it with your ear.
Tricky spellings,
They're really easy now!
Hear, ear, hear, ear.
Tricky spellings,
They're really easy now!

I love a piece of pie.
I love a piece of pie.
Tricky spellings,
They're really easy now!
Piece, pie, piece, pie.
Tricky spellings,
They're really easy now!

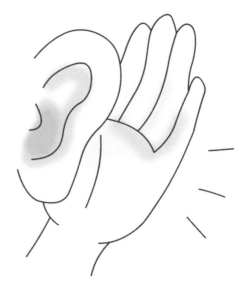

What would wear a hat?...
What, hat...

Find eight in height and weight...
Eight, height, eight, weight...

An end is found in friend...
End, friend...

Tricky tricky spellings!

JELLY

Using the song

★ Listen to the song (track 43) and join in with the male voice, spelling each word and saying it at the end of each verse.

★ Make a set of letter cards and choose five children to stand facing the class, each holding a card to spell the singular word. Two more children stand behind the child holding the 'y' card, one holding an 'i' card and the other an -es card.

★ Ask the class to perform the last line of the singular verse. The child holding the 'i' card swaps places with the 'y' and the word is completed by adding the -es card to the end of the line so that the whole of the plural word is displayed.

★ Repeat this for words in the third and fourth verses.

★ Perform the whole chant with the backing track (track 44).

Extend the activities

★ Working in small groups ask the children to compose new versions of the chant to perform to the backing track using other words with a 'y' ending which change to -ies in the plural, eg, poppy, story, lady, baby, city, bully, ferry, cherry. Each group can make a set of letter cards for their performance. They will need to decide on the rhythm of the different spelling patterns to fit in with the beat, eg,

Beat:	1	2	3	4
	L	A	D	Y
	ST	O	R	Y

What you will need

- A set of lower case letter cards: j, e, l, l, y, i, es, p, a, r, t, y, i, es
- For the extension activity: paper and pens for additional letter cards

TEACHING FOCUS

- Plural spelling rule: change 'y' to 'i', add -es

JELLY

J E L L Y   J E L L Y.
Red jelly, green jelly, orange jelly, wobbly jelly.
J E L L Y   J E L L Y.
Ends with double -ly.
Jelly!

J E L L I E S   J E L L I E S.
Red jellies, green jellies, orange jellies, wobbly jellies.
J E L L I E S   J E L L I E S.
Change 'y' to 'i', add -es.
Jellies!

P A R T Y   P A R T Y.
Street party, tea party, dinner party, birthday party.
P A R T Y   P A R T Y.
Ends with -rty.
PARTY!

P A R T I E S   P A R T I E S.
Street parties, tea parties, dinner parties, birthday parties.
P A R T I E S   P A R T I E S.
Change 'y' to 'i', add -es.
Parties!

MELODY LINES

ALPHABET SONG

PHONEME SPOTTER

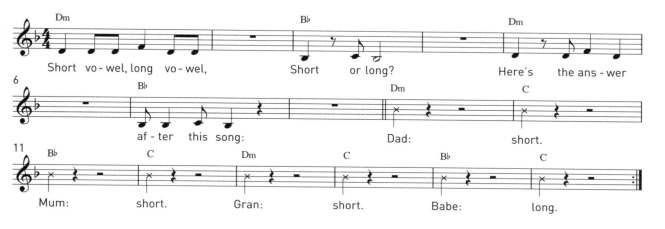

Short vo-wel, long vo-wel, Short or long? Here's the ans-wer af-ter this song: Dad: short. Mum: short. Gran: short. Babe: long.

SPELLING HOKEY COKEY

You put the let-ter t first and then the let-ter r too, You fi-nish with the let-ter y and give a yoo hoo hoo! You put them all to-ge-ther and you wait and see, What will the new word be? Oh, we can spell a new word, Oh, we can spell a new word, Oh, we can spell a new word, t - r - y spells try, you see.

51

SILENT LETTERS

SNAP, CRACKLE, POP!

HUBBLE BUBBLE

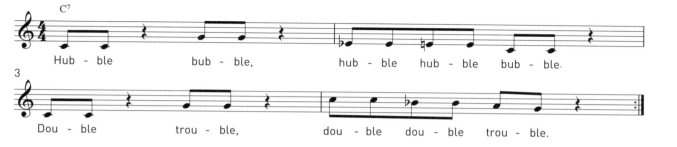

ANIMAL SYLLABLES

SINGING SPELLING © HELEN MACGREGOR & STEPHEN CHADWICK 2011, A&C BLACK PUBLISHERS LTD

BUSY KITCHEN

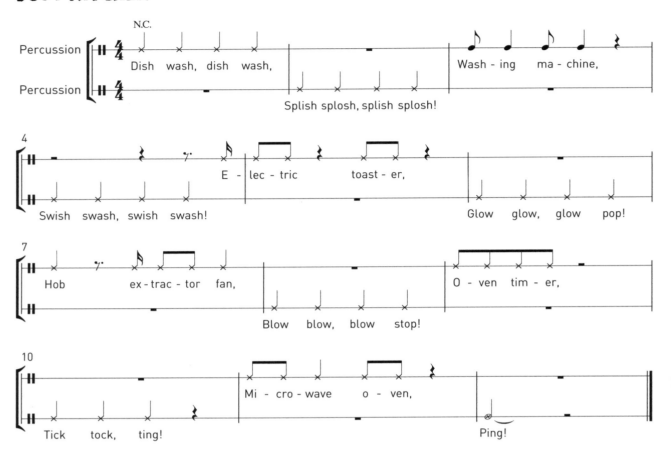

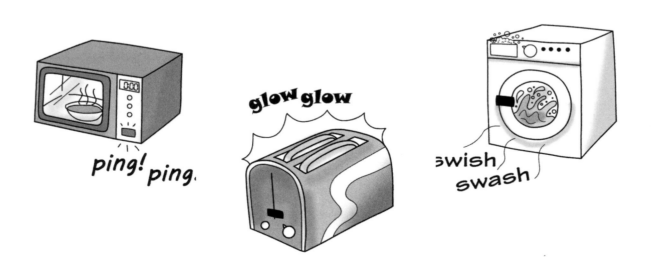

EVERYONE

F	C	Gm	C

Ev-'ry-one, ev-'ry-bo-dy, ev-'ry-where, Ev-'ry day, ev-'ry

night,_____ Needs shel-ter from the cold,__ food and

wa-ter, It's a ba-sic hu-man right._____ No-one, no-

-bo-dy, no-where, In the day or the night, Should be a-fraid or hurt, or feel that

no-thing In life can e-ver be bright. Oh yeah!

Ev-'ry-one, ev-'ry-bo-dy, ev-'ry-where, Ev-'ry day, ev-'ry night.

LOOK, WRITE, COVER, WRITE, CHECK

When you want to learn the way to spell a cer-tain word,_____

Sing this song and use this plan, the best I've e-ver heard: Look, say, co-ver, write and check.

(Don't for-get to check it!) Look, say, co-ver, write and check, I'm sure you won't re-gret it!

SINGING SPELLING © HELEN MACGREGOR & STEPHEN CHADWICK 2011, A&C BLACK PUBLISHERS LTD

RHYME RAP

Rhyme, rhyme, lis-ten to the rhyme, Stay cool and keep in time.

Rhyme, rhyme, lis-ten to the rhyme, Stay cool and keep in time.

I hear with my lit-tle ear, Some-thing that rhymes with cat.

Hat, rat, fat and splat, Words that rhyme with cat.

FEEL OKAY

Don't grum ble if you stum ble, Don't grum ble if you stum ble, Don't

grum - ble if you stum - ble and ev - 'ry - thing's a jum - ble, If

you step in a pud - dle, or get your-self in a mud-dle, Don't grum-ble! Don't grum-ble!

Why don't you... Just have a lit - tle gig - gle? Gig - gle gig - gle.

Don't let it nig - gle. Nig - gle nig - gle nig - gle. Give your toes a wig - gle.

Wig - gle wig - gle. Give your toes a wig - gle. And you'll feel o - kay!

SINGING SPELLING ©HELEN MACGREGOR & STEPHEN CHADWICK 2011, **A&C BLACK PUBLISHERS LTD**

CINDERELLA

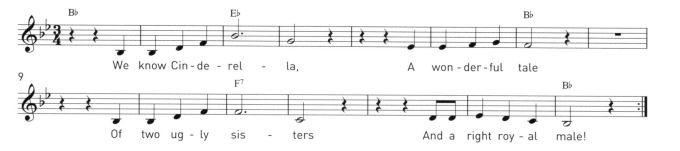

We know Cin-de-rel — la, A won-der-ful tale
Of two ug-ly sis — ters And a right roy-al male!

QUESTIONS

I won-der if earth-worms play foot-ball, Deep un-der the ground, in a hole?
D'you think that they e-ver have play-time? Their goal-keep-er could be a mole!
Ques — tions, ques — tions, I dream them up when I'm in bed, in
bed. Ques — tions, ques — tions, They buzz all a-round in my head.

PAST AND PRESENT

Show us what you're do-ing to-day, Do-ing to-day, do-ing to-day,

Show us what you're do-ing to-day, She's read-ing a book.

Ev-'ry sen-tence should have a verb, A do-ing word, yes, that's a verb,

Ev-'ry sen-tence should have a verb,__ And read-ing is pre-sent tense.

RECORD-BREAKING FOOD

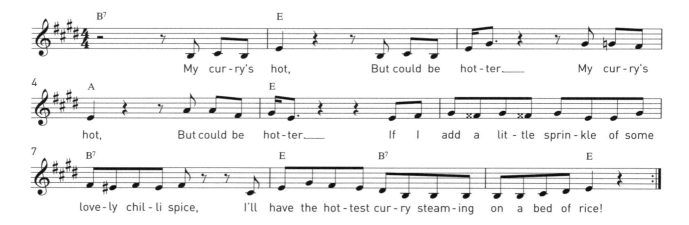

My cur-ry's hot, But could be hot-ter.___ My cur-ry's

hot, But could be hot-ter.___ If I add a lit-tle sprin-kle of some

love-ly chil-li spice, I'll have the hot-test cur-ry steam-ing on a bed of rice!

DING DONG

My bro-ther and I like to ar-gue, We ar-gue all day long. My

Mum says: 'Here they go a-gain – Ding-dong, ding-dong, ding-dong!' Yes, I

do. No, you don't. Yes, I will. No, you won't. Yes, I

do. No, you don't. Yes, I will. No, you won't.

STICK LIKE GLUE

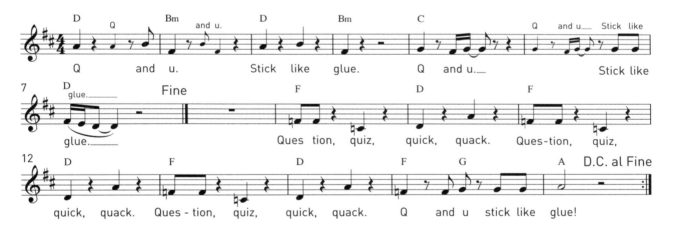

Q and u. Stick like glue. Q and u.__ Stick like

glue.__ Ques-tion, quiz, quick, quack. Ques-tion, quiz,

quick, quack. Ques-tion, quiz, quick, quack. Q and u stick like glue!

DOUBLE TROUBLE

WORDS TO REMEMBER

SPELLING TRICKS

JELLY

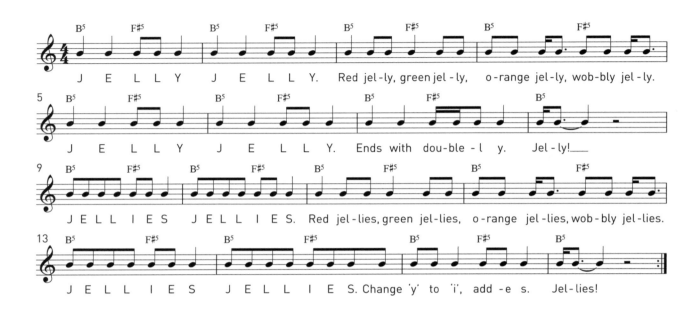

J E L L Y   J E L L Y.   Red jel-ly, green jel-ly,   o-range jel-ly, wob-bly jel-ly.

J E L L Y   J E L L Y.   Ends with dou-ble-l y.   Jel-ly!___

J E L L I E S   J E L L I E S.   Red jel-lies, green jel-lies,   o-range jel-lies, wob-bly jel-lies.

J E L L I E S   J E L L I E S. Change 'y' to 'i', add -e s.   Jel-lies!

ear

hear

wear

hat

pie

piece

quiz

question

weight	what
friend	height
eight	end
quick	quack

SINGING SPELLING ©HELEN MACGREGOR & STEPHEN CHADWICK 2011, A&C BLACK PUBLISHERS LTD